Anima

Thousands of years ago
all animals were wild.
Then some were tamed to give us food,
like milk.

Some were tamed to pull heavy loads.
Many were tamed to be our pets
and our friends.

Many animals are still wild,
and they live where
they have always lived.

Pet animals are tamed and live with us
in and around the house.

We can have animals like cats, dogs, rabbits and guinea pigs as pets.
These pet animals are called *mammals*.
Mammals are covered with hair or fur.
They have four legs.
They have warm blood.
Mammals give birth to live babies and feed them on milk.

Pet animals used to hunt for their food when they lived in the wild.
But now that they are tame,
we need to feed them every day.

Pets need milk or water, too.
And they need space so they can exercise and stay healthy.

Some large animals make good pets.
Horses and ponies need grassy paddocks and exercise, every day.

Calves are good pets and need milk.
So do lambs.
You can teach lambs tricks.

Birds like budgies, canaries, parrots and hens are pets, too. They used to live in the wild.

Birds are animals,
but they are not mammals.

They have feathers,
two legs and two wings.
Their bones are hollow and light
so they can fly.
They lay eggs, and then baby birds
hatch out of the eggs.

Pet birds need to be kept in cages.
Then they are safe from cats or dogs that might try to harm them.
Birds like to eat seeds and plants.
They also need water to drink.

Other animals make good pets, too.
You can keep turtles or goldfish
or tadpoles in a bowl or tank of water.
You must keep the water clean
and feed these pets.
These animals are not mammals or birds.

You could have a really unusual pet, like an axolotl.
Watch your finger – they bite!
You might even have a sea-horse for a pet.

Many wild animals live in zoos.
Animals in zoos need people
to care for them.

So zoo-keepers feed the animals every day
and keep their cages clean.

We need to look after . . .
animals that help us,
animals in zoos,
and all our pets.
And sometimes we need to look after
wild animals, too.